CRACKING
THE ACTING CODE
A Practical Step By Step Guide To
Becoming A Professional Actor

SABRINA M. REVELLE

TAJA V. SIMPSON

The Actor's Life Publishing

Copyright © 2017 Cracking The Acting Code

ISBN – 13:978-1-62676-823-9

Sabrina M. Revelle

Taja V. Simpson

Table of Contents

INTRODUCTION

While traveling down Broad Street, in Philadelphia one day, a voice randomly popped in my head.

"You're an actor", it said.

I looked around.

"Me? I asked.

"Yes, You!" it replied.

And for some reason, I believed it.

From that day forward, I made the decision to follow my intuition and set out towards this newly formed, grandiose dream in my head. I registered for the "Adult Theater Program" at the then famous Freedom Theater and stayed open minded to where the universe was steering me.

Shortly after, a local designer asked me to walk the runway of his fashion show. Now, being all of 5 feet 4 inches, I am nobody's fashion model, but staying open, I said yes and walked right into the next opportunity. The host of the event was a guy by the name of Marc Holley who, after meeting me, was convinced I needed to audition for a theater company being created by well-known radio personality, Tiffany

Bacon. However, the audition was the very next day, all the way across town and at least an hour to get to on public transportation.

"Oh, no, thank you", I quickly replied, "That is way too far to travel by bus". But he insisted.

"I really think you should come", he urged, "and if you do, I'll take you home". I remember my intuition, saying "Ok", and so began my acting career!

I performed with the Headline theater company for about a year. During one of those nights, a director by the name of Jamal Hill was in the audience and asked to meet me. We spoke briefly after the play and he stated he had a project he wanted me to work on. From there, I went on to work in two independent films with him.

All the while, I was studying computer science and was well on my way to becoming a code programmer. But after my first semester at Cheyney University, I received another message.

"This isn't for you. You belong in Los Angeles".

This time, I didn't question my intuition. I simply trusted and began planning my move.

Once I got to Los Angeles I realized just how *green* I was. Not only was I vulnerable to the business, I was also in a new state, a new place, alone...without any family or support system. Trying to navigate and understand a new land, while simultaneously going after a career I knew nothing about, was extremely difficult. I struggled with depression and my esteem was dropping daily, hitting brick wall after brick wall, until eventually I didn't any longer. After five years of learning this business, I began to *get* it. I finally began to understand how this place called "Hollywood" works. But, I've always wondered: what if I had a mentor? What if someone who related to my struggle, sat me down and plainly said *"these are the steps you need to take"*? Where would I be? Frankly, saving five years of "wasted" time.

It is our hope that this guide will do just that for you. Allow myself and Taja to be your mentors for this business.

- Sabrina Revelle

Growing up, I used to watch movies, learn the lines, and act them out in great detail to the pleasure of my family. My favorite movie at the time was "The Last Dragon." I had no idea that what I was doing was called "acting". For my cousins and I, it was simply "pretend". We would say, "Hey, wanna play pretend?" From there we made up games and songs with movie lines. My favorite game was, "Finish that line", using a snippet of a famous movie quote.

There weren't any acting classes in Lake Charles, Louisiana, nor in the surrounding areas, that could cultivate my skill-set. Instead, I focused on my studies and sports, from basketball, softball, volleyball, cheer and dance to track and field. At 16 years old I graduated high school and was ready to start my college journey. I finished at McNeese State University in Lake Charles and immediately moved to Houston, Texas. After about a year and a half in Houston, I decided to try my hand at acting and signed up for Gary Chason's Casting Director Workshop. It was a four week intensive that ended with a big showcase in front of agents and managers. When it was time for my scene to go up, I was relaxed and ready. For me, it was like "playing pretend" with my cousins. By the end of the night I had won three awards: Best Actress, People's Choice and Best Scene. It was the first time anyone had ever won that many awards and that gave me the confidence to really pursue my passion.

I then auditioned for my first short film and booked the lead role. That made me really believe I was onto something. I took another class with Gary Chason and he suggested I move to Los Angeles. Little did he know that I was already thinking about making that transition. He gave me the confirmation I needed to just go for it!

The thing is, I didn't know anything about the business and I thought as long as I had an agent I would blow up and be a star. But little did I know, that was not the case. There were so many elements of this industry I didn't know and everyone just assumes you should know what to do. Anytime I asked a question to my peers or industry professionals I was made to feel less than due to my lack of knowledge. I mean how was I supposed to get the knowledge if no one wanted to share? Many people I came across weren't as forth coming with information as I expected. I had to figure it out through a lot of trial and error. That's why writing this book was so important to Sabrina and I. We wanted to share our knowledge so you won't have to go through what we went through.

-Taja V. Simpson

There is a huge demand and influx of people craving for information about this field. We have written this book to offer the type of guidance we wish we had prior to moving and pursuing a career in entertainment. Every time an episode of a TV Show or movie we were on was aired, we would get so many calls, text, and emails of various people asking the same thing. "I want to get into acting, where do I start?" After spending countless hours on the phone with aspiring artists, we realized the busier we get, we wouldn't be able to help as many artists on a one-on-one basis. So *Cracking The Acting Code: A Practical Step by Step Guide To Becoming A Professional Actor* was born. This is our way of giving back and sharing the wealth through knowledge. After reading this, you will be on the path of success!

First Things First

Know Who You Are

If someone had pulled us to the side when we first got to LA and said the key is "Knowing Who You Are". It would've saved us a lot of heartache, hard work and money invested in the wrong directions. Knowing "your type" or what you "appear to be" is extremely important.

If you ask yourself the question, "Who Am I?" I'm sure you would be able to speak about your background, parents, and siblings, and describe them in great detail. You could recall different memories – good and bad, and talk about all types of experiences that have shaped you into the person you've become. However, knowing yourself not only includes all of that but also respecting your core values in life; your beliefs, your personality, your priorities, your moods, your habits, your body and your relationships. Understanding your strengths and weaknesses, your passions and fears, your desires and dreams. It means being aware of your eccentricities and idiosyncrasies, your likes and dislikes, and your tolerances and limitations. Remember you're a person first, actor second.

When you play a character in theater, TV or film, you should know your characters as well as you know yourself, so you can just exist, live and be. That doesn't happen out of the clear blue. As an actor you have to plant those memories and backstory, to give your character a sense of purpose and the only way that is achieved is by putting in the work. Take time to get to know yourself, find out what makes you tick and that will make life easier when building characters.

Just because you feel and all your friends agree that you're the nicest guy or gal on the block doesn't mean that's what you'll audition for. Your physical appearance has a lot to do with what you'll go out for and ultimately book. Unless you are Meryl Streep or Johnny Depp. If you look like the Big Scary Cop, Bodyguard, Bouncer or the Quirky Red-head girl next door or the sexy bombshell then that's what you'll be going out for. We know, we know we're all magnificent actors and we all can play anything our imaginations can think of. Hollywood is the land of make believe, right?! However, this is show BUSINESS. Emphasis on business, if you want to succeed you'll have to be able to view yourself objectively and in an honest light.

Don't get me wrong, we all can defy the odds! We really can!! Take Sabrina for example, she is very young and sweet looking to the naked eye, buuuut, her energy and presence says something completely different! Lets just say "she ain't the one to mess with" hahahaha! So sometimes your appearance is not going to match what you give off. If this is the case for you, you will have to choose whether you are going to only play your essence, your look, or both. Sabrina made the decision that her strength is what stands out the most. So while she looks sweet and innocent what she succeeds at is the strong-fierce type. But she wasn't about to let that stop her from missing out on commercials or teen roles so she worked on playing up her sweetness and naivety. We must be honest though, the roles she's booked as a giddy-sweet teen are way less than the strong-fierce types. Once you really do the soul searching that is necessary to figure out what your type is and stick to that, you may find your opportunities can seemingly become slim but don't fret, by doing this you'll actually focus on quality vs quantity. This laser focus will open up everything YOU are right for! We'll get into HOW you can REALLY find out what your type is a little later on.

Taja will be the first to tell you that knowing what she knows about herself today gives her the backbone she needs to approach any role with confidence. However, it wasn't always like that. Taja remembers being in acting class when the teacher would ask questions about the character's backstory and think to herself "Wow, I've never asked myself these questions". So, she treated herself as a character study and got to know herself inside and out. She took it upon herself to know the difference between the shy girl that she felt she was and the "I got this" woman who others saw whenever she walked into a room. Sounds simple enough, but it took a good deal of time for Taja to truly grasp her type because she didn't really understand who she was as life experiences had lowered her self-esteem. On top of that what she saw on TV made her think when you are on camera "you must look pretty". This caused her to treat auditions as "go-sees", which are really modeling auditions. She would strut into the room looking like, well, a model. The role could have been for Pine-Sol, but for some reason she would always have on heels and a full face of makeup. It was only when she read an interview with Nicole Kidman talking about being in the film "The Hours", where Nicole mentioned she had to stop caring about looking ugly on camera that Taja finally GOT IT! She realized she had to first be okay with who she was before giving herself over to any character in any genre. She made the decision to discover her core values and little idiosyncrasies that made her who she was and to develop characters with that same approach. Knowing who she is has allowed her to gain more confidence in the characters she creates. Understanding how other people saw her, and what she was giving off, ultimately helped her define her "type".

HOW TO FIGURE OUT YOUR TYPE

It is very important to have a clear sense of who you are when you walk into a room and what that means in terms of the roles you can audition for. Believe it or not, this is one of the biggest mistakes actors make. So please, we beg of you, take the time to figure out your type or, as often referred to, your "brand". We suggest you wait to start labeling yourself until you have completed professional acting training. That initial training is vital because:

1. Acting classes and workshops expose you to a range of characters you might be right for, but you've never considered.
2. Professional Commercial and Theatrical on-camera classes will give you a great way to objectively see and study yourself.
3. Improvisation classes will teach you to trust your instincts and help overcome any fears so you can be authentic and present.

When starting out, most Industry Professionals -- Casting Directors (CD), Directors, and Producers -- aren't aware of you or your talent. If it isn't an open casting call where you get to walk in and show them what you got, they will be calling you in from a picture, your "headshot". So let's all vow to be realistic with ourselves so we can get in the room and book! Look in the mirror, take a picture and really look at yourself. What do you see? HONESTLY?? Begin to research, see if you can find "your type" on the screen, i.e. TV, Film and the Stage. Now, Theater is obviously a little different in the sense that "type", and "age" doesn't always matter. They're more willing to make you up in costume to "look" the part if you bring the character to life! We want to be very clear, Our aim is NOT to limit you from becoming the next Meryl Streep or Johnny Depp. But if you're going to pursue that then you better have all your materials (headshots, reels, resume, postcards, website, etc.) represent the versatility you can play. What we ARE saying is, be smart about your career and play towards your strengths FIRST. Once you've gained some worthy credits in this industry THEN branch out to stretch your acting muscle.

A really great way to figuring out how you're seen by others and what your potential type could be is a method Sabrina learned and utilized from the marketing coach Dallas Travers. To use this method you would send an email to your family, friends, teachers, associates, industry professionals, etc. asking them to describe your essence and acting style. This will allow you to gain a wide perspective from those who've known you all your life to others who may have only seen you perform once. The people who've known you all your life may see things others may not but you'd be surprised at what is consistent in the responses you receive. If you happen to receive adjectives you feel are very different from one another, take a moment to research them as we're sure there will be similarities. For example energetic, powerful, and extraordinary are all synonyms for "intense", so maybe you have an intense acting style and give powerful performances that lend to a leading man or leading lady. Let's say you received "intelligent", "eccentric" and "meek", chances are you may be the quiet, quirky and dare we say nerdy type. Using the adjectives you received from this technique, coupled with your "look" will give you a well-rounded point of view to discovering your type.

Email Example:

Email subject: Need Your Help PLEASE...Describe My Essence and Acting Presence

Hey Jane or John Doe,

Would you mind helping me out?? What do you feel my essence is? When I walk in the room what do you feel or get from me? Be honest even if it's something you may find negative or offensive...

Example: When you walk in a room, I feel your essence is...

> Strong, Fun, Giddy,
> Meek, Seductive, Intimidating

If you have only seen me perform then please send at least two adjectives to describe my acting presence...

Example:

> Denzel Washington: commanding
> Johnny Depp: one-of-a-kind
> Edward Norton: surprising
> Cate Blanchett: fearless

.........and so on and so forth. I'm focusing on branding myself and I really need your honest feedback so I can figure this out. Thanks a bunch for your time and help with this! I value your opinion and expertise!

Sincerely,
Jane or John Doe

The moment Sabrina pressed "send" she was truly frightened of what she would get back as she grew up being told she was too opinionated and should stay in a child's place. She began to view herself and her opinions in a negative light. The way we view ourselves can play a huge part in what we <u>are</u> and what we are <u>not</u> booking. In a matter of minutes she was receiving the most invaluable and eye opening information she could ever receive. So we urge you not to worry, send this email, shaking if you have to! What you will get back will be absolutely enlightening, career changing and AMAZING!!!

We hope we've convinced you that <u>Knowing Who You Are</u> is very important because your essence is what you will add to each performance. As Taja always says, "Bring yourself to the role", which is what Sabrina likes to call putting your "stank" on it...the good smelling kind! We truly believe this is what will set you apart from any other actor performing the same exact role. We encourage you to BE YOU whoever that may be. Live fully, truthfully and unapologetically. This will serve you not only in your acting career, but your life.

Learn Your Craft

Get In A Class

Now that you have an idea of what your "type" is, you can use that knowledge to decide on the perfect course for you. To be an actor it is necessary to have a wide spectrum of skills, and the ability to understand comedy, drama, improvisation, emotional reactivity, use of voice, and physical expression. Acting can also command the use of stage and screen combat, observation, dialects, accents, and even emulation. Many actors train in special programs or colleges to develop these skills.

Obtaining an acting education from a university is an amazing way to study the craft, but is not necessary. However if you choose to attend a university depending on what course you take you'll walk away with a deep rich knowledge of the history of Theater or Film. You'll not only be studying acting but also all of the other required general classes like math, english, science etc. Albeit, the time and money required to complete a 4 year course may be a challenge for some. If you feel this is you but still wish to be classically trained or have a solid style of acting in your arsenal, there are specific techniques that you may want to look into. These programs will give you a formal way to study the techniques without the extra general courses and normally range between 2 - 4 years but typically require less time and money than a university. Selecting the proper technique that will help you develop your skillset is one of the most important decisions you will need to make. Here are some of the popular methods and techniques.

Constantin Stanislavski

One of the greatest acting teachers of all time, Constantin Stanislavski's work signaled a shift in 20th century acting and inspired a whole new generation of techniques and teachers. In addition to changing the face of acting worldwide, Stanislavski's Moscow Art Theatre was at the forefront of the naturalistic theater movement in the Soviet Union and in Europe. His approach incorporates spiritual realism, emotional memory, dramatic and self-analysis, and disciplined practice.

Lee Strasberg's Method

An actor himself, Lee Strasberg's method was inspired by Stanislavski's system and the Moscow Art Theatre. His "method" encourages actors to magnify and intensify their connection to the material by creating their characters' emotional experiences in their own lives.

Stella Adler

Stella Adler was the only American actor to study with Stanislavski himself, and developed her own "method" built on the work of Stanislavski and Lee Strasberg. Adler's technique differs from Strasberg's in that it emphasizes imagination in addition to emotional recall.

Meisner Technique

Sanford Meisner developed this unique approach in the 1930s, after working with Lee Strasberg and Stella Adler at The Group Theatre. Like Stanislavski, Strasberg, and Adler before him, Meisner taught his students to "live truthfully through imaginary circumstances". His approach is an imminently practical one. His famous repetition exercise, in which two actors sit opposite each other and respond in the moment with a repeated phrase, breaks down overly structured technique and builds openness, flexibility, and listening skills.

Michael Chekhov

Stanislavski's star student, Michael Chekhov developed his own acting technique after exile from Russia brought him to Europe and the United States in the late 1920s. Chekhov pioneered a psycho-physical approach to acting, focusing on mind, body, and a conscious awareness of the senses.

Uta Hagen

In addition to her work as a Tony Award-winning actor, Uta Hagen was a beloved teacher at New York's Herbert Berghof Studio and authored the best-selling "Respect for Acting" and "A Challenge for the Actor". Her popular technique emphasizes realism and truth above all else; "substitution" (or "transference") encourages actors to substitute their own experiences and emotional recollections for the given circumstances of a scene.

Suzuki Method

Developed by internationally acclaimed director Tadashi Suzuki and the Suzuki Company of Toga, the Suzuki Method's principal concern is with restoring the wholeness of the human body to the theatrical context and uncovering the actor's innate expressive abilities. A rigorous physical discipline drawn from such diverse influences as ballet, traditional Japanese, Greek Theater, and martial arts. The training seeks to heighten the actor's emotional and physical power and commitment to each moment on the stage. Attention is on the lower body and a vocabulary of footwork, sharpening the actor's breath control and concentration.

Viola Spolin

Viola Spolin is considered an important innovator in 20th century American Theater for creating directorial techniques to help actors to be focused in the present moment and to find choices improvisationally, as if in real life. These acting exercises she later called "Theater Games" and formed the first body of work that enabled other directors and actors to create improvisational theater. Her book, "Improvisation for the Theater", which published these techniques, includes her philosophy, as well as her teaching and coaching methods. The book is widely considered the "bible of improvisational theater". Spolin's contributions were seminal to the improvisational theater movement in the U.S. She is acclaimed to be the mother of Improvisational Theater.

A technique class is great for beginners and also seasoned actors to return to when they need to brush up on their skills. It is a class that focuses on the skill-set rather than putting together the performance. All of these techniques will give you a specific structure to follow in order to live fully in your characters and will carry you through drama and comedy. There are some teachers who teach a mixture of these techniques and some who don't teach a famous "method" at all but rather their own structure or technique that they have created themselves. All can be taught by some really amazing instructors and some not so great instructors. Some teachers tear you down to build you up and some don't feel that is necessary. All of the techniques and teaching styles work for someone. Keep in mind, there is no ONE correct way to learn acting. Choose the right one for YOU.

There are also classes, workshops and intensives you can take that are not restricted to two or four years of study. They may run for a month or ongoing till whenever you wish to stop, i.e. Acting 101, Intermediate Acting, Master Class, etc. In any class you choose, just be sure you are learning how to break down a script, create your environment, work off your scene partner, develop a character and how to bring yourself to your work *(put your stank on it).* A great class definitely will and should challenge you! Most of the times when you hit breakthroughs in class you're really hitting breakthroughs in your personal life, so don't be afraid of your vulnerability or of feeling "exposed". Class is supposed to be and should always be a safe place. With that said, make sure it is THE place for you by researching the class thoroughly and auditing the class whenever possible. Try not to take classes that do not offer audits unless they're reputable with REAL success stories as proof that they in fact offer great training that breeds results. Even with success stories try to interview the instructor because your connection to the actual teacher is what's going to make or break what you walk away with. Think about it like dating, there are a lot of great guys & gals out there, all with great qualities that we're looking for but we do not and will not "click" with all of them. There are only a few "magic" will be created with and those are the keepers! The same goes for your teachers. Here are some great questions to ask any potential Teacher:

Where and what did you study?

Can you tell me what methodology you teach? (If not already known)

What is your teaching style?

What are you looking for in and from a student?

What is your ratio of working actors (people who make a living as actors who took or are taking their course)

Will you actually be my teacher? (or is it someone else under you)

If not, how do you train your teachers?

Do you teach the business of acting as well as the art?

As Stuart Rogers (a great acting teacher here in LA) says "Press the teacher and make sure that you like their answers.

Remember if the teacher can't stand up to scrutiny, they probably have something to hide!"

Constant training is a necessity. Whether it's an ongoing class, studying and coaching with an experienced actor-friend, ongoing private coaching or private coaching for a specific audition. Even if you have years of training you should always be looking to hone your skills, remain emotionally available and ready for the opportunities that come your way. Professional athletes don't graduate from training and neither do we. If you're not working consistently on film, TV or stage you should try to exercise your "acting" muscles whenever possible.

Apart from the University and College or Method and Technique courses we've been speaking about, you also have classes that cater to a specific skill or type of acting. We call them "tools". These classes consist of but not limited to audition technique, cold reading, commercial acting, improv, sketch, acting for multi-cam sitcoms, dialects and accents, voiceover, stunts, etc. Typically these classes would come after a solid background of acting training. For instance, Audition Technique is NOT an "acting" class and most auditioning course instructors will tell you that you must already have acting training to attend. Auditioning is a skill separate from acting ("the work"). Meaning how you play it on set or on stage, 9 out of 10 times will be different from how you've auditioned it. It's a skill within itself to master. Most actors can do "the work" but when in the audition room under the pressure of needing to be great, well let's just say some of us crack!! It's like trying to run before you've even crawled. There may be some astonishing exceptions to that rule but exception is the key word, rules are made for the majority. So this is something you should invest in but not right away. Learn your craft first! Then add these different "tools" to your toolbox. However, if for example you know your goal is to ONLY work on commercials, voiceover or improv then by all means begin with the course that matches your goal. Allow your dream of where you want to be, coupled with research, intelligence, and common sense guide you.

It doesn't matter if you're in the big apple or "timbuktu". Research, Research, Research! If it sounds too good to be true, it probably is! Stay clear of these chain model schools and big traveling seminars where none of their students move on to actually work in the industry. A lot of them are designed to sell you a dream, take your money and leave you guessing. Learn from our mistakes and do extensive research on the seminars and classes you are interested in. If you are in a city or town that doesn't offer any great classes and you wish to travel to a nearby city or one of the larger markets (NY, LA, ATL, CHI, etc.) to take a course and you can afford to do so, DO IT! Just be sure it is in fact a reputable school, teacher or casting director teaching the course so you are learning from the best, get your money's worth, and potentially make good connections. Ask other actors who have already taken the course what they felt about it. Your fellow actors are one of your top gauges for getting into a great class, then the "professional work" actors are booking from the class and the MOST important gauge is what YOUR own intuition is telling you. Listen clearly to all three and make your decision.

Let's Talk Genre

Understanding The Different Styles And Tones Of Acting

N ow that you're submitting to projects and you get the call or email that you have an audition, to prepare, you'll receive what the industry calls sides. The term "sides" has been in the entertainment industry dating back to the time of Shakespeare. Rather than give the entire script to every actor in a play, actors got only the lines and cues for their specific roles, literally just their SIDE of the scene. This saved on paper, and the limited number of complete scripts prevented rival theater companies from stealing each other's scripts.

Currently, the word "sides" is used to reference the part of a script given to actors for use in an audition and are usually available in advance. How much in advance depends on the project. Just as Shakespeare and his competitors guarded their full scripts, today's commercial, film and television productions still use sides for auditions to reduce costs and prevent scripts from being leaked to the internet, ruined by spoilers, or stolen outright. It's also common practice that writers will create "audition sides" that are completely different from the script you'll receive once you've booked the role. Keeping a lid on storylines are very important.

Now that you have the sides for the audition, it's great to know the type of project you're auditioning for and by that we mean the TONE of the production. When reading a script or sides, try to monitor the tone of the writing and the narration of the story. Pay attention to the writer and how they write. The definition of tone is the way the author expresses their attitude through their writing. It can change very quickly, or remain the same throughout the story.

There are many different types of productions, and each of them has a different TONE. For instance, Situational Comedies (Sitcoms - *Friends*) are very different from a Procedural Drama (*Law & Order*). It is your job as an actor to understand the differences and master how to work your craft for each genre. If you get an audition for a show you do not watch, try to find the show and watch a few episodes to get its tone and pacing. If it's a pilot, this can be a bit trickier because the show hasn't yet aired therefore you have no reference to go off of. Do everything in your power to get as much information about the pilot so you can make educated choices. Have your agent or manager get the pilot script for you and if that's not possible or you still don't quite understand the tone ask or have your agent ask casting directly for the tone and a show reference. We can't stress enough, truly understanding the tone and pacing of a show is very crucial. You can have a phenomenal audition but if you're not within the style of the show the casting director may unfortunately think you "aren't right for the part".

Most TV shows are broadly defined as either half hour comedies or full hour dramas (episodics).

TELEVISION

COMEDIES are generally broken down into these sub genres:

WORKPLACE
(e.g. The Office, Parks and Recreation)

FAMILY
(e.g. Family Guy, Blackish, Modern Family)

ROMANTIC
(e.g. Younger, Dharma and Greg, Mike and Molly)

ENSEMBLE
(e.g. Friends, Big Bang Theory)

DRAMAS are generally broken down into these sub genres:

PROCEDURALS

Stories that originate from problems being solved according to prearranged procedures, typically mysteries, cop or detective shows. These are typically standalone, book-ended stories that can be viewed non-sequentially and still make sense. They might have a B or C subplot running through a series, but usually not enough to break the flow of a random viewing order. (e.g. The Mentalist, CSI, Criminal Minds).

MEDICAL

Stories originated from medical settings (e.g. Grey's Anatomy, House, Nurse Jackie)

LEGAL

Stories originated from legal settings (e.g. Law & Order, Suits, The Good Wife, Scandal)

SOAP

These are highly chronological, continuous stories that must be viewed sequentially to make sense. (e.g. "The Bold & The Beautiful", "Days of our Lives" "General Hospital" "Young and the Restless").

CHARACTER DRIVEN

A hybrid of a standalone and chronological series (e.g. Grey's Anatomy, The Good Wife). The A Story tends to be procedural and the B story continually character based.

EVENT
These are highly chronological, epic shows and tend to be grandiose in nature (e.g. Game of Thrones, Once Upon A Time, The Tudors).

COMMERCIALS

COMPARISON OR UNIQUE PERSONALITY PROPERTY

In this type of commercial, you as the actor advocates for one brand over the other. The advertiser wants to see that your experience with their brand or product is happier than with the competition's brand or product. The desired objective of this type of commercial is to instruct the viewer of why a certain product or service is better than other products or services. It generally focuses on differences with other brands as opposed to the consumer's need or want for the product. For example, a Samsung commercial that tells you why their phone is better than the iPhone.

PROBLEM THEN SOLUTION

Since most commercials are designed to move viewers emotionally to buy a brand, your job as the actor in this type of ad is to experience the problem as you would in real life. For example, you'd hate to have an irremovable stain on one of your favorite clothing items, so this ad might highlight the difficulty in removing a stubborn stain with ordinary detergents. This is the problem. Then they will show how easily their brand removes the stain in quick time. This is the solution. Again, here your experience as the actor in the ad is what will move the viewer to try the advertiser's brand over the competition. There is always a need or problem that will require a solution and these two types of commercials offer different ways of doing so. Showing the consumer the need or problem and of course providing a solution with their product is a straightforward and simple type of ad. Another example, a tech company might show how a new app takes away the problem of long lines at the grocery store by offering a home delivery system for groceries.

DEMO AND EXEMPLARY FORMATS

In this type of ad, the product is usually the hero. In cases where an actor is used, subtlety goes a long way. You may be required to show the benefits of the product but not to upstage it, meaning do not become the focus. Any type of "household item" television commercial will give you a sample of the Demo format. You've seen this type of commercial many times for vacuums, glass cleaner, dish washing soap, the list goes on. Sometimes companies will use real people as opposed to actors to demo the product and capture their reactions on camera. It shows you the effects of the of the product using before and after images, describing the product's features and how it works. The Exemplary form of this commercials focal point is more on the after effects and the benefits the consumer has experienced from using their product. Think of a skin care ad, you see how happy the consumer is now that their face is zit free.

TESTIMONIAL AND PARODY OR BORROWED FORMATS

Testimonial ads are simply what the name implies, a testimony from an actor or real person sharing a positive experience with the viewer. In testimonial ads where an actor is used, "naturalness" is always favored over "hard sell". In other words, speak as though you are talking to a friend and sharing your experience of the product. This type of ad is also popular in direct mail advertising. A real and happy customer may be offered an incentive to share their experiences in this type of commercial. For example, a matchmaking company will use the success of happy couples to share how they fell in love using their service. The Parody or Borrowed format "borrows" its theme from a popular film or TV show. Commercial spots like these typically prank trending hot topics from reality shows or news reports. For example, a company could spoof a news segment to bring you breaking news of their new product.

BENEFIT CAUSES STORY AND THE SYMBOL WITH ANALOGY EXAGGERATED FX BENEFIT

The Benefit Causes Story format will usually have a comical tone. It does not take itself too seriously because it shows an improbable thing happening through the use of the product. This type of ad usually plays on a fantasy that the user may have and shows that something unbelievable will happen as a benefit of using the product. For example, drinking Red Bull gives you wings. The viewer knows that this, of course, is too good to be true but the exaggerated effect can be comical and leave a lasting impression in the consumer's mind.

CHARACTERS OR CELEBRITIES AND ASSOCIATED USER IMAGERY

Using characters and celebrities format is how companies use that person's popularity in the hopes viewers will want to purchase the product because of them wanting to be more like that celebrity. For example, think of a water ad that has a mega star saying it's the only water they drink to stay hydrated and keeps their skin looking nice. If you are a follower of that celebrity, you may want to purchase that water for the same benefits. That's the hope of the company, to woo the audience. If a celebrity is out of budget, other local familiar faces will be used as a feasible replacement. Associated User Imagery format uses unknown characters or common stereotypes that the advertiser wants associated with the product. For instance, an advertiser may have a group of people laying by a pool, checking into a prestigious hotel or enjoying an upscale activity. Both formats target the aspirational viewer who would love to live that lifestyle and be more like the celebrity or stereotype.

FILM

ACTION

Action films are filled with just that: Action! They generally have big budgets to include the high energy stunts, fight scenes, car chase sequences, explosions, fires, etc. The storylines are often the good guy versus the bad guy that allow audiences to escape to a world of non-stop motion. Examples: Wonder Woman, X-men, Transformers, Star Wars, The Matrix, The Fast and the Furious franchise.

ADVENTURE

Adventure films are comparable to the action film genre with lively storylines or exotic locations. These types of films can consist of conventional serialized films or historical content. Examples: Pirates of the Caribbean, The Mummy, Jurassic World, Lord of The Rings.

COMEDIES

Comedies are simple, effervescent storylines that are created to incite laughs. These types of films generally emphasize and heighten the situation with the language, action, relationships and characters. It involves numerous forms of comedy such as romantic comedies, black or dark satirical comedy, screwball, spoofs, slapstick and parodies.

Examples: Pretty Woman, Borat, Shaun of the Dead, Hail Caesar!, Scary Movie Franchise.

CRIME

Crime or gangster films are centered on the mischievous works of criminals, mobsters, bank robbers, gangsters, or characters who aren't law abiding citizens. They tend to steal or murder their way to get what they want. Examples: The Godfather, American Gangster, Gone Baby Gone, Gotti.

DRAMAS

Drams are of the largest film genre that usually have serious character and event driven storylines. The context of these realistic settings use stories involving profound character development and interaction. Generally these films are not fixated on special effects, comedy or action. Examples: Moonlight, Lion, Kramer vs. Kramer, The Social Network.

EPICS

Epics typically consist of dramas, historical dramas and war films. Think of this genre as a period picture that can also share components of adventure films. Epics take an historical or imaginary event, mythic, legendary, or heroic figure, and add an extravagant setting and costumes, including high production values and amazing musical scores. Examples: Troy, Lord of the rings, Spartacus, Titanic.

HORROR

Horror films are constructed to scare and invoke fear in the audience while captivating and entertaining us with the often used alarming, shocking finale. Horror films offer a wide range of styles from psychological thrillers to CGI monsters and villains. Examples: SAW franchise, The Amityville Horror, IT, Nightmare on Elm Street.

THRILLER

Thriller films also referred to as suspense or psychological thrillers includes a wide range of genres that usually evoke suspense and anticipation. These genres can include fantasy, action, adventure, and sci-fi. Horror and Thriller films share a close bond due to the anxiety building nature of both. Examples: Get Out, Sixth Sense, Memento, Michael Clayton.

SCIENCE FICTION (SCI-FI)

Sci-fi is a genre that combines science and fiction, and is usually based in the "what if?" of scientific fantasy. These films are often inspiring and groundbreaking. The narrative includes heroes, aliens, faraway planets, impossible quests, improbable settings, great dark and shadowy villains, futuristic technology, unknown forces, and extraordinary monsters (things or creatures from space), either created by mad scientists or by nuclear havoc. Examples: ET, Star Wars, The Matrix, Interstellar.

MUSICAL AND DANCE

Musical and Dance films accentuate full musical scores or song and dance routines throughout the film. Typically the musical or dance performance is combined as part of the narrative, or the films are focused on various combinations of the music, dance, song or choreography. Examples: LA LA Land, The Five Heartbeats, Grease.

WAR

War or anti-war, films can deal with the dismay or agony that a war brings to the specific time or period of the film. You will generally see actual combat fighting on land, sea, or air as the primary event, plot or environment of the story of the film. War films are often paired with all the previous genres listed above. Examples: Dunkirk, Saving Private Ryan, The Hurt Locker, Red Tails.

WESTERN

Western films are one of the oldest, most long lasting genres with very distinguishable plots, elements, and characters typically including six-guns, horses, dusty towns and trails, Cowboys, and Indians. Examples: The Magnificent 7, Django, The Hateful Eight, The Good The Bad and The Ugly.

Take Your Best Shot

Headshots

Now that we've covered Understanding and Knowing your type in Chapter one, and you've figured out who you are and what characters you represent well in this industry, it's time you obtain headshots that capture your essence, represent you and or those characters in the best way possible. When this topic is brought up, so many questions follow and this chapter will give you all the tools you need to get that amazing, dynamic, stand out from the crowd shot.

Your Headshot is your most important tool as it is the very thing that will get you IN the audition room. Whether you're starting out in this business or an actor who is submitting headshots and you're not getting nearly enough auditions, it is time to get or update the most important calling card of your career; The HEADSHOT.

You want that opportunity? Well, you better have a good headshot! In color, NO black & whites, that's old school! That doesn't mean you have to pay a torso and foot for them, especially when you're just starting out and you're not represented by an agency yet. It's best to spend less because a potential agent or manager may have recommendations for your type along with a list of photographers.

When spending less, be sure not to forfeit quality. Do not go to Sears or JC Penny for headshots. All photographers are not created equal. There are a bevy of different types of photography; Portrait, Fashion, Beauty, to name a few. Headshot photography is a separate niche. When making your selection, be sure to choose a great HEADSHOT photographer. This is something we can't stress enough. Selecting someone who does not typically shoot headshots will totally do you a disservice.

You want to choose a photographer whose style matches best with who you are or the character you want to represent. Sometimes this means multiple photographers; maybe you like one for its gritty, realistic, down to earth look for your theatrical dramatic shots and the other for its stylized clean-cut commercial shots. If you shoot both styles you'll want to be sure the photographer's body of work represents the two styles adequately, or select two completely separate photographers. We want to be clear, this is NOT about pretty pictures or glamour shots. This is about bringing out YOUR essence and personality. How are you when you're the quirky teen, the heartthrob, the nerd, the boss, the victim, the mother, etc? You should be thinking of something in every shot that correlates with the character you're representing so it shows through your eyes! Casting directors choose your headshot to come into their office for an opportunity because your EYES say something very specific to them that fits the character.

With that said, let's talk makeup. Makeup artists are almost always available through your photographer for an additional fee. If you have your own makeup artist, be sure they're great with Headshot photography. However, it's not always necessary. Here are some simple tips you can do yourself:

KIDS AND TEENS

No heavy make up for children ever, no matter their age. These pictures are not for pageants or to make your child appear older. They are to enhance your child's natural look and features.

CHILDREN

4 - 8 years old can benefit from moisturizer and lip balm only.

OLDER CHILDREN

9 - 12 years old can use moisturizer, light foundation, light blush, ever slightly tinted lip balm or gloss and CLEAR mascara. Remember these are not pictures for pageants. They are to show your child in their best light. When choosing blush and a tinted lip balm or gloss, choose colors that simply enhance the natural color of your child's cheeks and lips not change them completely. Boys can also benefit from moisturizer and a slightly tinted lip balm.

TEENS

13 years old and above can definitely apply a full face of makeup but just as the adults it should be kept fresh and natural. Moisturizer, foundation, concealer, blush, tinted lip gloss, mascara. Depending on your child's type and characters they represent you may want to build mascara & eyeliner as you go. Start out with only mascara, add eyeliner, then go heavier on both, and finally if shooting a goth character, even heavier. Teenage Boys can also benefit from

foundation, concealer and tinted lip balm. Of course this all depends on your child's skin, blemishes, breakouts etc.

Let this be a case by case decision. If your child has clear skin and their features already stand out go the simpler route, use your best judgment.

MEN

Here are some items you can bring to the shoot with you; oil blotting paper, translucent powder or the very inexpensive paper towels. These are needed for when you become too shiny; you'll blot the excess oil off your face. If you want a little more polished look go to your nearest make up store that offers assistance with choosing colors and pick up a tinted moisturizer or light powder NOT a heavy foundation. This will cover your blemishes and make you appear more even toned all around. It's also good to have handy for auditions and shoots.

Again think of who you are, the type you're representing. You can do both by bringing your tinted moisturizer to the shoot with you and save your more polished look for last so you won't waste time having to take off the makeup to do the rest of the shoot. You simply build as you go. Same as if you're shooting a beard and a non-bearded look. You should start with the beard, then shave to a goatee and finally to bare face. This way you can get more looks from your session but be sure to discuss this with your photographer so they know how much time to allot for your shoot.

WOMEN

Don't go so heavy on the makeup that the casting director doesn't recognize you at the audition. This is not Instagram! Apply your makeup as you would on your best day. Do not do a super heavy smoky eye if you're not portraying a party or club girl that's possibly into drugs. Always make sure your eyes pop but think about what and who you're representing. This could also mean no makeup at all. Your imperfections are what you may want to accent if the character you're shooting is homeless. Get the drift? Less is more. Simple coverage and colors that accent your best features and bring out your eyes are best.

CLOTHING

Keep it simple! NO LOGOS, NO LOGOS, NO LOGOS! NO PROPS, NO PROPS, NO PROPS! Make sure there aren't any distractions in the photo that will take away from you. You don't need to show casting you love adidas and that you can hold an umbrella. This includes huge necklaces, big earrings, (unless it fits your character) graphic t-shirts, busy backgrounds, or anything that will take away from what's important in the shot, YOU! As we keep drilling into you think of who you are, what you represent and what characters you're portraying. A few examples: **Business**: button down with Suit Jacket or blazer, **Detective**: T-Shirt with jacket or blazer, **Young Mom**: Cardigan with tank, **Dad**: Button down with V-neck sweater or plaid shirt. **Teen:** T-Shirt possibly jean jacket, **Gangster:** ribbed tank (better known as wife beater) **YOU:** a simple shirt, tank, t-shirt, flannel or whatever represents you best. This is not a strict list. These are only guidelines but keep it simple. You do not want to distract from your face and most of all EYES. Choose colors that make your eyes pop. We always say, when in doubt, don't do it. If you're not sure on multiple character looks, take simple headshots that represent you as a person. One smiling commercial and one serious theatrical.

Framing for Headshots are typically shoulder, chest or waist up. NO extreme close ups or full body shots. You do not need full outfits. The only exceptions for full body shots are if you're a fitness model, swimsuit model or dancer. These will most likely be used for commercials & print modeling with the occasional "hot girl or hot guy" breakdown for theatrical auditions.

The focus of your headshot should be YOU. The background should not pull focus from your lovely face. You want to be the only thing that stands out in your image and anything that takes away from you is distracting, i.e. flowers, people, cars, etc. Some of the best headshots have a blurred background which makes you more of the focal point. This is known as "high depth of field".

Ahhhh, and now for lighting. Do you shoot in Natural Light (outside), Studio Light or both? We prefer natural lighting but be sure to choose what works best for you, your skin tone and your type. The lighting in headshots should not be too dark, too light or have extreme shadows. When shooting for Commercial looks, these tend to be brighter and are generally perky in nature. While Theatrical looks tend to be on the darker side and are more serious in nature.

You want to be sure your photographer knows their stuff; lighting, shadows, backdrops, etc. to bring out the best in you. When viewing a photographer's body of work, investigate to ensure they shoot and light your type, ethnicity, gender and age well. It may sound weird but we found a lot of photographers were great for men but not for women, great for children but not for adults and great for Caucasians but not African Americans. So try not to be persuaded solely by great headshots and think this is IT. Take your time to see if those few shots represent you. If you really love a photographer's work but they don't have any pictures that represent you, ask them if they have any samples they can send you. Often times they've shot with people recently but haven't updated their sites yet.

If you aren't sure always ask, ask, ask before paying your hard earned money. Here are some questions you can ask your potential photographer:

Do you shoot with high-depth of field?
(This is when your background is blurry so that you are the ONLY focus in the pictures)

Will the image quality be shot in 300 dpi?
(This is so your pictures come out crisp and clear when printing)

Here are the type(s) I'm going for, is this something you feel you can help me achieve?

Will you vocally guide me through the process according to which character and look I'm shooting to be sure we represent that character well?

What is your shooting style and environment like?
(Can I have music playing? Is there a changing station, mirror for applying and changing makeup between looks? etc.)

How many photos do you take?

How many photos will I receive?

How many, if any, come retouched?

Some of these can be answered on their websites however,

you still want to have a conversation with your photographer so you know you're both on the same page and there is good professional chemistry between the two of you.

Beware of Agencies and Companies running scams. Especially in cities or towns where acting and modeling is not a big industry. We would rather you pay to travel to a photographer who's the real deal than give your money to a fake. It's one thing for representation to say, "Hey, you really need some shots that will capture your essence better. Here are a few I recommend. Please send me your choices as well and I'll give you my professional opinion to help you narrow it down to one." It's another thing for agencies, companies and schools to actually reach out to you and show interest but REQUIRE you to shoot with "said photographer" for a ridiculous amount of money! Don't forget Google and The Better Business Bureau are your friends when it comes to researching if a company is a scam or in fact the real deal.

We live in this new age with a thing called social media. If you don't have an actor community where you live, find up and coming actors online and if you like their Headshots ask them what photographer they used and go from there. If you do have an actors community, of course, ask your fellow actors for recommendations. There are also sites like www.Backstage.com, www.ActorsAccess.com, www.LACasting.com, www.CastingNetworks.com, etc. that will offer a free list of photographers. If you attend Casting

Director workshops or have a good relationship with a few, ask them, they're the ones choosing so they know best. While they're just people and some of their pet peeves may differ, overall the good Casting Directors will be able to steer you in the right direction for a great photographer.

COST

There are great photographers at every range. We feel a typical range is anywhere from $200-$700 but can go all the way up to $2000. If you have the funds to pay $2,000 for headshots with THE top headshot photographer in the game and it won't ruffle a feather in your pillow when you try to sleep at night, then by all means do it. We personally think it's highway robbery for headshots. If we were fashion models looking for modeling shots for our portfolio we'd understand but headshots, com'on. However, typically you can see a quality difference between the low end and high end photographers.

There are tons in the low-middle range who will provide you with great shots to get you in the room and on the road to booking. Some even offer one look deals; upcoming photographers do this a lot. One look for $50-$100. Check their work, be sure they're good.

Headshot sessions can be very pricey and even more so if you aren't comfortable in front of the camera. Do you not like how you photograph sometimes? Or does it take you a while to warm up? Maybe this will be you or your child's first professional photo shoot? Well, just like anything else in this business, practice makes perfect and this would be the time to do practice shoots and trade for pictures. Practice shoots are literally just that, practice. Grab your phone or camera and a buddy to snap away while you work your angles, looks and characters. See what you like, don't like and what you may need to work on. It will make you more comfortable and prepared for your paid headshot photo session.

Trade for pictures (TFP) means you the actor and typically a new photographer make an equal trade. You're trading you and your likeness and the photographer is trading their photography. The photographer gets to build their Headshot portfolio for free while you receive potentially great headshots, also for free. Always be sure that you own your pictures and can do as you wish with them. We've found TFP very beneficial for headshots when we first started out.

STEPS TO FINDING TFP

www.ModelMayhem.com - geared towards modeling but you can find photographers on there looking to branch out into headshots

www.purpleport.com - both professionals and amateurs use this site to arrange shoots.

www.Craigslist.org - search "TFP" in your area.

Check your local makeup schools. They often look for models for their soon to be graduate students. But be sure the pictures you choose from this bunch are NOT the glamour shots but the more natural, realistic shots. Be willing to give the school and artist what they need but ask ahead of time if it's ok to take a few headshot style photos with natural make up before doing the more glam shots.

Facebook and LinkedIn are other great places to find photographers for TFP. Utilize their search engine for acting, photography, makeup and industry groups or forums by searching keywords -- photography, headshots, test shoots, collaborations, etc.

There are so many scams and unfortunately not all people are good people in the world. Always, always, always take someone with you to a shoot for safety reasons. Especially when meeting a photographer for the first time and (or) it's in a location you don't quite trust, i.e. Hotel rooms, parks, allies, places with not so good reception, etc. If you must go to a shoot alone please notify a family member or friend where, when and whom you'll be shooting with. This isn't to make you fearful but just the opposite, to prepare you with knowledge of how to stay safe and aware.

You will need to update your headshot every one to two years. For kids and teens, possibly every year or even every 6 months depending on how fast they grow or change. So it's good to have a reasonably priced photographer if you have kids in show biz. Of course if you change drastically, lost or gained a significant amount of weight, going from long to super short hair or vice versa, dying hair, etc. you will need to change your headshot even if it hasn't been a year or two yet. Keep it up to date so you're doing a good job at representing you and so you don't waste the Casting Director's time. You need to look like your headshot when you walk into their office.

Most important, when choosing your photographer trust your gut. You will know your top photographer once you see their work and have a conversation with them. Remember your pictures have to really pop! Your headshots will be seen by the casting director on their computer in a tiny thumbnail photo, it MUST stick out to be among the chosen few!

For a list of photographers, see the resource section. For Headshot examples, see the next page.

Photographer name listed under each photo

Bradley K. Ross   Will Catlett   Bradley K. Ross   Bradley K. Ross

Peter Konerko   Peter Konerko   Pancho Moore   Alisha Peats

Maya Darasaw   David Muller   Naiyah Scaife   Peter Konerko

Natalie Young   Jonathan Marlow   Paul Smith   Brandin Shaeffer

Stephanie Girard   Stephanie Girard   Maya Guez   Mike Quain

Be Proactive

Self Submissions and Creating Your Own Work

Self-Submissions are when you submit yourself to a project(s) you hope to be called in to audition for. You either do this by mailing a hard copy of your headshot (which is very rare nowadays) or submitting your headshot electronically to the casting director via an online submission site. You can self-submit whether you have an agent or not. How are you able to do this? Well it depends where you live but in the major markets (LA, NY, Chicago, ATL) there are online submission websites where you create a free profile, upload headshot(s) and pay a monthly fee to submit to projects on the site. We will share some reputable sites a little later on. If you can't afford the monthly submission fees, be sure to still create a profile on each site, uploading as many free pictures that are allowed. Casting Directors visit these sites from time to time scouting talent they may not already have in their pool of actors for their projects. When setting up each profile, be sure to select the option to have breakdowns emailed to you regularly.

When submitting to any breakdown, project or CD, be PROFESSIONAL! DO NOT submit for a 6 year old African American female if you're a 65 year old white male. You may literally laugh out loud at that statement but we have run castings for our own indie projects and you will be surprised at what people do. Now, we get it, those actors simply wanted to be seen by the CD. However when a CD is working on a project and you submit to a role that you do not fit, you are creating MORE work and adding to the stress they may already be experiencing looking for the right actors. Please make their jobs easier by being professional and efficient, do not send in tapes for every single role the CD puts out on breakdowns, only submit to roles you are right for. You want to remember it's the longevity you're aiming for not just one role or project so have respect for the process. You are building a professional relationship with each CD you submit to.

On most of the submission sites, you have the option to choose multiple regions you wish to receive breakdowns from, i.e. LA, NY, ATL, etc. When submitting to a region you do not reside in be prepared to put yourself on tape. If the breakdown calls for a "local hire", production is looking to "hire" someone who lives in the area. So just know if you are not really a local hire living in that area, you will have to cover the cost of airfare and lodging, unless the breakdown states otherwise.

Self-Submissions are especially great for an actor who has minimal to no credits. You are able to submit to TV, theatre, student films, indie projects, commercials and occasionally the big block-buster film. Once you begin booking projects you will now be able to build your resume and reel. Whether you're a newbie or a veteran, have an agent or not it's still a good idea to self-submit. It keeps your audition skills up to par and you active in your career. We've heard actors say they don't self-submit because it's their agent's job. Well, we say, this is your dream and you can't put 100% of your dream in someone else's hands. Your agent or manager gets paid 10%-20% of what you make so there job is only 10%-20% of the work. YOU must work the other 80%-90%. If you come across representation that tells you, you cannot self-submit you may want to think about if they're the right representation for you. Have a candid conversation with them, ask them why not, tell them what kind of quality projects you'll be looking to submit on and how you will pitch yourself so they can trust you as their client and trust that you will only be adding to your elevation. Remember they work for you not the other way around. Think about the level of agency and what they can offer you. If you feel their level of opportunities will be better in quality and quantity than what you can attain you may want to still sign with them. If that's not the case you may want to pass. You are your business, run it the way you wish coupled with the intelligence & experience of your agent.

Carve out time in your daily life to submit and do it with passion. Whether you get the audition or not, if sides are available, print them, study, prepare the scene and if possible put yourself on tape, even if it's only for a practice round. Watch it back and review your choices. This is one way you get to work on your craft daily without waiting for an audition. Practice makes perfect. The more you do, the better you will become. We all want our names to be uttered among the actors who are the best to ever do it. But it's going the extra mile that will truly make you stand out amongst the crowd.

Self-Taped auditions are the future of casting and the future is now. Typically you get a call from your agent or casting director to go into the casting office to audition. However, more and more often we actors are getting calls to self-tape. Now what exactly is a Self-Tape? This is when you tape yourself or pay a self-taping service to tape you performing an audition instead of physically going to a CD's office. Self-tapes should be treated the same way you would treat an in person audition. The only difference is the casting director is not in the room so your performance needs to be stellar because you don't have the luxury of getting feedback and adjustments.

You can also self-tape on your own. You don't have to wait to get the call. Being proactive is a great quality to have in our field. If you opt to get a membership with showfax.com (see resource section) you are then able to look under their "sides" tab for TV shows & films you want to be on and a character that fits YOUR type. Do NOT choose just any role, choose a role you're right for and put yourself on tape. If this is not a practice round, find a way to submit it to that project but DO NOT post it publicly on youtube, vimeo or any other website where it is visible to the public because the sides and script are confidential material. You should find out if you are capable to get to the CD or producers of the show before you take the time to put it on tape. Research CD's email addresses using google, imdb pro and if you begin to attend CD workshops they typically give their email and mailing addresses. If you have representation, tell them the show and role you're looking to put on tape and ask them if they're willing to send it over to the CD. As long as you're treating it professionally and you have a great chance of booking the role, your representation will most likely say yes! Again, be sure you're right for the role when self-taping an audition you have not been called in for. Do not waste the CD's time. You and your representations reputations are on the line.

HOW TO SHOOT SELF-TAPED AUDITIONS

All Self-Tapes are not created equal but there are a few industry standard rules you will need to follow. When receiving a self-tape request, sometimes casting may have you hold a sheet of paper with your name, height and agency, some may not. Others may have you do a tail slate, which means you will slate your name at the end of the performance instead of at the beginning. Some may want the slate as a separate file. Casting may ask for a full body shot and then change the frame to a medium shot for the slate. It all varies. The point we're making here is to please follow the directions explicitly. You want to make sure you're putting your best foot forward.

Here are the industry standards of self-taping:

LIGHTING

If you don't have studio lighting, that's okay, natural lighting is always great. If you have a window in your home that brings in a lot of light, that may be a good spot to shoot. Just be sure you are well lit. It doesn't have to be studio quality but we need to be able to see you. If you're at home, and you don't have good natural lighting or studio lights, get creative. If you have lamps, position them so you are better lit.

SOUND

CD's need to be able to hear you. Please do your best to cancel out any loud background noises, so it isn't distracting to your performance. You may want to go the extra mile and purchase a microphone, i.e. boom, lapel, or mic attachment for your phone but it's totally not necessary. Just make sure whatever recording device you use we can hear you clearly.

BACKGROUND

A plain blue backdrop is preferred. However any plain solid colored background or wall is acceptable. If for some reason you are unable to use a solid colored backdrop or wall and your only option is to use a background with furniture, etc. then make sure your performance is on point so the background doesn't overshadow you and your performance.

FRAMING

The frame is what the camera sees for the shot. You want to make sure we can see your lovely face and your reactions in the scene. Typically one of the three frames are requested; head to shoulders, head to chest or head to waist. If you are using your cell phone to tape, please make sure you are using the phone turned in the horizontal position. No vertical submissions will ever be allowed. Set your camera up on a tripod so there's no shakiness especially if you're using a camera phone. If you don't have a tripod, maybe use an antigravity phone case that sticks to multiple surfaces or just prop it up with a few books, a windowsill or something of the sort. You shouldn't break the fourth wall by looking into the barrel of the camera, unless instructed to do so, or taping a reporter or anchor role. Don't forget to make sure you are in focus. Every camera is different, be sure to check the instructions on how to set the focus on your camera or phone. The idea is to create the best framing that would allow casting to see and hear you clearly.

Self Tape Example: (Blue Background & Good lighting, Framing):

READER

Do your best not to have a bad reader as it could make your audition suffer. If you have any actor friends that can read with you, call them up and have them assist you. If not, really work on the scene with your reader so he or she is comfortable with the dialogue. Have your reader stand or sit beside the camera so that your eyeline is close enough to the camera without looking into the lens. Again the objective is to see you, your emotions and performance without breaking the fourth wall. Keep in mind, your reader is closer to the camera than you are, the microphone will pick up their voice louder than yours. Have them speak a bit lower than you to not overshadow your performance. BUT don't get caught in the trap of matching their voice level, keep your voice at the level you naturally would in the scene. If you do not have a reader physically available to be in the room with you, call someone, put them on speakerphone and tape your audition that way. Just be sure your eyeline is where your reader should be for the scene.

HOW MANY TAKES

Many people say different things about this but we will say to follow the breakdown of the character that's been given to you first, then if you feel you would portray the role differently, put an additional take(s) at the end of your tape. We can't stress enough, when sending multiple takes on a scene(s), be sure they are a completely different 'take' on the character.

If you don't have a professional camera or a cell phone, the SAG Foundation offers equipment rental for free or you will have to pay a self-taping service to film it for you. This option can get pretty pricy, it's best to invest in yourself and purchase some type of digital camera so you can stay ready.

A perk to having your own gear and setup is you can take it with you when you travel. That way you're able to put auditions on tape wherever you are.

CREATE

Get creative! In this day and age you don't have to wait to be discovered. The days of an A&R department in the music business are over, they're looking for artists who are somewhat established. The film and TV industry is no different. Think of YOUR type (which you discovered in Chapter 1) and or that character you've always wanted to play and create a project around that. You can go the traditional route by creating a feature film or a short film and enter it into festivals hoping it runs the festival circuit. Write a play, put it up at your local theater and try to get industry guests to come out to see you. Those options are still tried-and-true and while they are great they may take a little bit more money and effort to produce. The beautiful thing about the age we're in is most of us are walking around with everything we need in our pockets, that's right, our phones. Social Media allows you to create short form productions and gives you a platform to showcase your content to a much broader audience. Here are some ideas; web series, one-minute monologues, reenacting scenes from your favorite TV shows and films. The options are endless. If you have other talents or skills like singing, playing instruments, dancing, stand-up, improv or sketch comedy, maybe even burping the alphabet or eyebrow dancing, you can post your clips for the world to see. Whatever you decide, make sure it's in line with what you wish to represent in the industry and do it with passion.

COMPETITIONS

Always be on the search! Nowadays the internet is connecting everyone especially in the entertainment field. Acting competitions are a great way to get discovered and seen by industry leaders, especially if you aren't in a major market and wouldn't typically have access to that kind of visibility. As always, be smart, aware and safe. Check the Better Business Bureau (BBB) and Google the company's name with the words "reviews" or "scams" (ex. "ABC Company Reviews", "ABC Company Scams"). Research the websites and competitions; are they asking you to pay for anything? How long have they been offering the competition? Who won the previous year? Research the winner using Google and other social media platforms. Make sure they're a real person, if they won a competition I'm sure they would post about it. Do the most research you can to protect yourself. New competitions pop up all the time so don't rely on the few examples we're sharing with you, always be on the lookout.

See Resources for list of competitions.

Let's Get Technical

Resume & Reel

Now that you have your headshot(s), it's time to create your resume. An actor's resume should list their experience along with any union affiliations, training, education, any special skills you may have and your physical stats (this is optional). Your resume should be clean and sharp just like a "professional" career resume. The difference is in the layout. Some things can be tweaked as you see fit perhaps to stand out a little, but for the most part the sections will remain the same.

Your resume will be one (1) sheet of paper, ONLY. When formatting your resume set the "ruler" on your document (in your program of choice) to 8"x10" to be sure that all of your credits fit on the page once printed. Your Full Name or Stage Name should go at the top of the page in a font size larger than anything else on the page, like a header. It can be placed center, left align or right align, it's your choice. Your contact info should be placed underneath your name or somewhere close by and should be in a smaller font than your name. Never list your mailing address and only add your age if under 18. If you have representation their contact information and logo should go there as well, either beside your name (opposite from where you've placed your name, i.e. if your name is left aligned your agency's can be right aligned), underneath your name, etc. Here is where you can choose what is aesthetically pleasing to your eye and the page. You want your resume to be professional so don't try to do too much. Industry Professionals need to be able to read your name and contact info clearly. You do want that call, right? So no super-duper fancy fonts. Instead, choose easy to read fonts like Arial or Times New Roman. The purpose of a resume is to show your credits in an easily readable format. Most of the time these will be read in the room as you're auditioning hence keeping it simple is best.

The sections that should be listed on your resume are: **"Film", "TV", "New Media", "Commercials", "Theater", "Training and Education" and "Special Skills".** Under each section you will list your credits (projects you have worked on thus far), with the exception of "Commercials". You should place "list available upon request" underneath the commercials section. The reason for this is because you don't want Mcdonalds to see you had a Burger King commercial when they're looking to cast their lovely new Big Mac commercial. It can be viewed as a conflict of interest. Only show your commercial credits when absolutely necessary. Keep an updated record separate from your resume to have it on hand when needed.

When listing the "type of role", do not use the character's name (Except for Theater). Instead, for Television, you should use Series Regular, Guest Star, Recurring, Co-Star, Under Five (you've had 5 lines or less), etc. For Daytime TV (soap operas) use Principal, Recurring, Day Player, etc. For Film you should use Lead, Supporting, Under Five, etc. If you're not familiar with these terms don't worry when you book the job you will be told in your contract what type of role it is.

Keep your resume current, credits must make sense; If you're a recent high school graduate it is okay to list your credits from school performances, however if you're in your 30's, there is no need to list the roles you played in elementary or high school. This comes across as amateurish. You don't have to list every single credit you've done. Again, it must make sense and it's okay to purge your resume when needed.

Do not list any background work; this is when you're in the background of the scene without any lines. If you don't have any experience, that's okay, don't be afraid to show all of the white space, be proud to only list your Training and Education. We've all had to start somewhere and there is nothing wrong with that. Whatever you do, don't lie about your experience or credits. It's unethical. This industry is very small and people always have a way of finding out.

When asked for a hard copy of your headshot and resume, you will hand them your headshot with your resume already stapled to the back, FONT side up. You want it stapled that way so when viewing your headshot they're able to flip it over and see your resume neatly on the back. Most times your resume is printed on

8 1/2 x 11 paper. Once stapled to your headshot (be sure all the words on your resume line up appropriately with the headshot) cut the extra paper that's sticking out beyond your 8x10 headshot so the headshot and resume are the same size (this is why you set your ruler to 8x10 when creating your resume so everything would fit once stapled and cut). If you have a paper cutter or go to a professional printing company you can cut or request to have your resume cut to 8x10. When cutting your resume, line it up with the actual headshot you'll be stapling it to, to ensure correct measurement, as you'll find not all 8x10 headshots are exactly 8x10. We wouldn't recommend printing your resume directly on the back of the actual headshot. As your bookings

increase your resume changes. Here are all the sections we talked about:

RESUME HEADER

Name, Union Affiliations (if any), **Your and/or Agency Contact Information, Physical Stats** (this is optional).

UNION AFFILIATIONS

SAG-AFTRA

Screen Actors Guild, American Federation of Television and Radio Artists is an American labor union representing approximately 160,000 film and television principal and background performers, journalists, recording artists and radio personalities worldwide.

SAG-AFTRAe

Represents the actor who is "eligible" to join SAG-AFTRA but hasn't yet.

EQUITY/AEA

The Actors' Equity Association is an American labor union representing the world of live theatrical performance (Theatre), as opposed to film and television performance which is represented by SAG-AFTRA.

If you're not a member of any union, just keep that part blank.

CONTACT INFORMATION

List your contact information and/or agents' or managers'.

PERSONAL STATS

Your height, weight, hair and eye color.

If you are a singer or do musical theater, you should list your vocal type in this section as well. Example, Voice: Soprano.

Your Name

SAG-AFTRA/AEA

My Agency	Height:	5'10"
111 Agency Row	Weight:	165
Los Angeles, CA 90210	Hair:	Black
800.555.1234	Eyes:	Brown

Your Name
800.555.1234

Height: 5'10"   Weight: 165   Hair: Black   Eyes: Brown

CREDITS

List the **Name of the Project,** followed by the **Type of Role, Network or Production Company** and **Director of the Project**.

You can list the credits in a chronological order or in order of size of the role. Either way, don't ever add the date you worked on it.

THEATRE

List the Name of the Show, followed by your Role, Theatre Company and Location of the Production.

Add the Director if he or she is well known. Otherwise do not include the Director.

If you have extensive theatre experience, you can provide a partial list which showcases your biggest roles to date.

THEATER (Partial List)

Rocky Honor Show	Riff-Raff	Big Time Theater,	Los Angeles, CA
Little Shop of Horrors	Seymour	Carousal Theatre,	San Jose, CA
Harvey	Elwod P. Dowd	Reader Theatre Group,	Astonia, NY

TRAINING AND EDUCATION

List all of your Acting Training and Education. Performing arts schools, college study, improv troupes, acting classes, etc. You will notice (Current) listed below, that lets the casting director know you are currently training with this acting coach. Only add the graduation year if it is within two years of completion. Otherwise, you will age yourself.

TRAINING:

Sandra Seacat (Current)	Sean Study	Los Angeles
Larry Moss	Master Class	Los Angeles
BFA Theatre	University of Maryland, College Park, MD	

SPECIAL SKILLS

This section can be used as a great conversation starter. Sit and think about what your special skills are and list the things that would be considered "special". If you work in a specific profession, like news, it may be good to add "TelePrompter Experience". Or if you are a real life doctor, by all means put that too. It's the last part of your resume and the only part where it's great to add a bit of humor. Also add your dialects and accents to this section. This doesn't have to be a long list, but whatever you put down, be honest about your level of skill-set and be able to perform it if called upon.

You can also take a look at the special skills section of the actor sites mentioned in the Resources section at the back of the book. The lists of special skills on those sites may jog your memory of all the cool things you can do.

SPECIAL SKILLS:
Stand-Up, Singing, (Tenor), Dialetcs, (Australian, British), Amateur, Contortionist, (Go Ahead, Ask me!)

Voila! You have an acting resume!

Jane John Doe

SAG-AFTRA/AEA

Artists Agency	Height: 5'6"
Agent Name	Weight: 120
555-123-4567	Hari: Brown
agent@agentagency.com	Eyes: Green

TELEVISION

The Good Doctor	Recurring	Dir. James Smith
Game Of Thrones	Guest Star	Dir Joel Zwick

FILM

Carts's Life	Lead	Dir. Lena Roberts
Rejoice	Lead	Dir Rachel Archie

THEATRE   (full list of avaible upon request)

Chisholm	Lead	WA Theatre Company
Colorblind	Lead	Meta Theatre Company

COMMERCIALS

List Avaible Upon Request

TRAINING

Scene Study	Aaron Speiser	Los Angeles, CA
Improvisation	J.W. Myers	Idiot Central, LA, CA

SPECIAL SKILLS

MC & Host, Teleprompter, Director, Screenwriter, Cheerlearding, Dancer -
Hip-Hop & Jazz, Boxing, Comedic Timing, Modeling, Track, Softball,
Swimming, Roller Skating, Bowling, Basketball, Volleyball.

DIALECTS

Southern, British

Let's Get Rep'd

How To
Obtain Representation

All of the chapters thus far have led to this final one. Getting an Agent. Everyone wants one, but does everyone need one when starting out? The first question people tend to ask you when you say you're an Actor is, "Do you have an agent?" It's a sense of pride to respond, "Yes, I do", but it takes time to get there. Don't be ashamed of not having one right away. When posed with that question, state proudly, something to the effect of: "I'm building my experience and reel right now in preparation for a great agent". Training, preparation and experience are key before an agent will take you on as a client. Think of it this way, if you want to be a doctor, you would have to go through a residency program (training and experience) prior to treating patients on your own. There is no way around it, agents treat their clientele the same way. Generally agents will not sign an inexperienced actor due to the fear that the actor will make the rep look bad in the audition room. Can you be trusted to do a good job and make your representation look good in front of reputable Casting Directors? Parents this goes for your children too. Make sure your child has the necessary experience and are ready for auditions before submitting them for representation.

Agent and manager roles are supposed to be different. An agent must work for a talent agency that is licensed by the state, which gives them the legal right to solicit employment for their clients and negotiate contracts on their behalf. Agents also must physically work out of an office. The average agent will represent a roster (a list of clients they represent) anywhere from 100 to 150 clients. The role of an agent is to submit and pitch you to projects and once you've booked a role, negotiate your contract. Agents are not allowed to take more than 10% of their client's earnings.

A manager does not have to be employed by a management company and can work on their own. Managers are not legally allowed to set up auditions or negotiate contracts. A manager's roster is way smaller than an agent's so they can provide personal attention needed for each client. Great managers tend to have less than 20 clients. A manager should manage your career schedule, photo shoots, come up with a detail plan with you regarding your look, type, what kind of work you wish to perform, and industry professionals you wish to be connected with, etc. Depending on their connections, managers should also set up meetings with those prospects to help build relationships for you in this industry. Their sole purpose is to provide guidance. However, in the real world a lot of managers do less of the personal priming and simply "act as agents" by submitting actors to projects in hopes of getting the actor the audition and booking the role. Yeah, everyone tends to turn a blind eye to the legalities, because at the end of the day, everyone wants to work. Just be sure whatever manager you choose you're happy with the service they provide you.

Managers are not restricted by a certain percentage but they tend to take anywhere from 10%-20% with the average being 15%. Don't be afraid to negotiate with managers for a lower percentage, especially if you're already represented by an agent. For example, there are instances where the actor will have a manager and two agents in different regions; one in LA and one in ATL. All three have agreed on splitting the commission equally receiving 7% from the actor for each and every job the actor books regardless of which representation in either region got the actor the opportunity. A contract like this was only agreed upon through negotiations, don't be afraid to ask. They may say no but hey it's worth asking.

If you sign with both an agent and a manager, just know you'll have to pay the agent on every project in the categories the agent represents you for, i.e. Commercial, Theatrical, etc. but a manager is not limited to a specific department of representation. You'll have to pay their commission percentage on EVERY project you book in the entertainment industry, i.e. Voice-overs, print, commercial, Theatrical etc. If you've self-submitted and booked the project on your own you STILL have to pay your manager and corresponding representation their commission fee.

TIP: If you book a self-submitted project tell your agent to negotiate the contract that way you don't feel slighted because they've actually worked for their percentage. Another way to feel better about this is to simply think about all the hours they spend on submitting and pitching you to no success. Your understanding of their level of work ethic (if they're doing their job) will have you wanting to pay them with glee and thanksgiving in your heart.

New actors tend to stick to one kind of rep, typically an agent due to not having the credits that would allow them to sign with the level of manager that can truly give them the personal attention mentioned above. However some do choose to go with a manager over an agent, but the idea is still the same: no sense in paying two people doing the same job. Of course there are newbies who come out the gate with two amazing reps. Chances are they had something those reps found saleable, i.e. they're an up and coming stand-up comedian that is making waves in the industry, they're a star in a popular web series, they were found in their prestigious college showcase like Yale, etc. OR they've simply used their superpowers and intention with the universe and voila amazing rep appeared, LOL. Nothing is impossible. Nonetheless, we're providing you with guidelines of how the industry typically works.

Remember all the tools we spoke about along the way; your headshots, resume, reel and online profiles? These will all be utilized to submit yourself to potential agents and managers in a bid to gain representation. It's important for you to know that Commercial agents are usually easier to attain, a little more lenient and will take on newbies as clients being that commercials are based on a look or type mostly. They're also a good way to sustain yourself financially while pursuing your film and television career. So it's a good idea to begin submitting to Commercial Agents first.

Theatrical agents (Film/TV) may take a little longer to obtain. Most good theatrical agents won't take on clients who aren't in SAG-AFTRA as the majority of TV shows and Films fall under this union. If you are curious about a specific agency, all legit agencies are listed here: www.agentassociation.com/. You may also want to pay to become a member of www.imdbpro.com to research agencies, managers and you can even get a peek at their rosters.

HOW TO GET REPRESENTATION

There are multiple ways to obtain representation but we find the best, cheapest and most effective way is through a referral. This could happen a couple of ways; an industry professional may be impressed by your work and refer you on their own accord or you may know a fellow actor who has reputable representation, ask them for a referral. It's a great way to be seen by the representation because they trust and respect the opinion of a colleague.

When submitting without a referral, you should always "target" your mailings. To do this, research agencies, develop a list of the ones you wish to target (submit to). Investigate each agency thoroughly by searching their client rosters and the productions their clients have previously booked. A couple of questions you may want to ask yourself:

Are the productions of quality?

Do you see network TV credits, theatrical releases or quality indie projects (projects that are produced outside of the major studio system)?

How many clients do they already have in your type or category?

Submitting to an agency that does not have your type puts you in a better position of being signed by that agent. If the agency only has one or two of your type, you may still want to submit. If it's three or more, we do not recommend submitting. When an agency already has three or more of the same type chances are the rapport and trust between client and agent has been established. The agent has more than likely submitted them to multiple projects and they have been auditioning, building rapport and trust with Casting Directors. Think about it, if you as the new client are being submitted with the reliable clients who already have the established trust and rapport, more than likely, the CD will call in the veterans over you. You're already in competition with actors at other agencies you do not want to be in direct competition with actors within your own agency. Your end goal is to have a list of agencies that would represent you and your type efficiently. For example, if you notice an agency only represents quirky, funky, punk rocker types and you fit in the fringe category, that's an agency you should add to your target list.

Now you are ready to submit to your target list. To submit via snail mail (although isn't used very often anymore), send a hardcopy picture and resume along with a cover letter in an unsealed 8x10 envelope large enough to comfortably fit both items without having to fold them. There are companies that make windowed envelopes so that your headshot will be seen directly without the agent having to open it. It's a nice addition but not necessary. If you have a demo reel include that too on a USB drive. Any and all items sent will not be returned to you. Hence why this way isn't used often, it can be very expensive. Visit each agency's website for submission instructions before spending any money as they may lay out in detail how they'd like to receive submissions.

When submitting via email, everything should be concise and easily viewable for the representation. The preferred method would be to use one of the profiles you created from the submission sites in the Resource section. These sites typically provide you with a custom link to your profile that will contain your stats, multiple pictures, resume and reel all in one place. If you prefer to send your materials attached to an email, send a personalized message with your headshot attached or as an inline file. The inline file will allow your headshot to be conveniently seen in the body of the email (check your specific email service on how to do so). However, beware not all inline files are viewable within all email servers. You may use Gmail, but the agent may use Outlook and your file may not show. (So we suggest you use your personalized link from one of the submission sites.) As previously stated make sure your resume is in PDF format before attaching it to the email. Your reel should be placed within the email as a link not an attachment. This is to make it easier on the representation. They do not have time to download hundreds of files from potential clients. To do this you can upload your reel to YouTube, Vimeo or the like (choose unlisted or private if you do not wish to have your reel public) and use that link.

TIP: When submitting, typically Pilot season (Jan - April) is not the best time to submit to agencies simply because it's extremely busy. Agents are hard at work for their current clients. It's better to submit before, (early December - mid January) or after (late April - early May.) Due to the constant changes in the industry, these dates may vary. Please do your research.

Email Example:
Little to no professional experience

Hi Agent Name,

My name is Jane or John Doe; I'm a funny, lovable, down to earth girl or guy next door type living in the Los Angeles area and seeking Theatrical / Commercial / Voice-Over Representation.

I've recently completed a two year acting program at the prestigious Professional Actors Studio and I am excited about this next season of my journey.

My resume is attached, you can **check out my reel here:** www.youtube.com/YourReel

I thank you for your time and look forward to hearing from and especially meeting with you soon!

Jane or John Doe
555-400-0313
Actor
www.JaneJohnDoe.com
www.imdb.me/janejohndoe

Email Example:
With Professional Experience

Hi Agent Name,

My name is Jane or John Doe; I'm an actor in the Los Angeles area. I've been booking some great work with my manager who's based in NYC. Most notably I'm a **recurring guest-star** on Nashville with a guaranteed 4 episodes which they keep adding to!

While my NY rep has been great, I'm based in LA so I'm looking for theatrical rep here in LA LA Land. I'm currently with BBR commercially and Atlas Talent for Voice Over.

In addition to Nashville which I've been shooting this and last month in the role of "George", my recent bookings have been:

Supporting role in "Oh Lucy!"
Co-Star on "New Girl" 4 National Voice Overs, Coca-Cola,
McDonald's, Honda and Avatar The speaking voice of
Tupac Shakur in "Straight Outta Compton"
 Supporting role in "Whiplash"

Also, because I sing, rap and play 5 instruments, I have an advantage with musical projects. Thanks for your time, I look forward to hearing from and especially meeting you soon!

Reel: www.youtube.com/YourReel

Jane or John Doe
555-400-0313
Actor / Musician / Writer
www.JaneJohnDoe.com
www.imdb.me/janejohndoe

Keep in mind these are just examples. Everything is interchangeable with your information; who you are, your experience and what you're seeking. In the sentence "I'm a funny, lovable, down to earth girl or guy next door type" we're using three adjectives and an archetype to describe the actor's "type". The archetype being "girl or guy next door", the three adjectives being "funny, lovable and down to earth". You should already know your type from chapter one. Be sure to use adjectives that capture what you exude the most.

Another way to obtain representation is by attending Agent & Manager Showcases. These typically consist of anywhere from 3-7 different agents or managers in a panel style setting, where each actor displays their talents by performing a scene or monologue and if the representation is interested they will contact the actor to schedule a meeting. This is the most expensive way to find representation as these showcases can run in the high hundreds to attend. We suggest using this avenue when you find that your top choice(s) from your target list are set to be there.

We are firm believers in the individual journey and doing what's right for you. We hope you've used this guide intelligently by allowing your intuition to guide you through the steps. You should be well on your way to a successful acting career.

Remember...Dreams don't work unless you do!

Sabrina M. Revelle
Taja V. Simpson

Resources

Photographers

Los Angeles

Bradley K. Ross
www.bradleykross.com
IG bradleykross

Brandin Shaeffer
www.brandinphotography.com/

Dana Patrick
www.danapatrick.com

David Muller (LA/NY)
www.DavidMullerPhotography.com
IG: davidmullerphotography

Joanna Degeneres
www.joannadegeneres.com

Jonathan Marlow
www.marlowphotography.com
IG: marlowphoto

Joshua Monesson
www.monessonphotography.com

Maya Darasaw
www.madworksphotography.com
IG: madworksphoto

Maya Guez
www.mayaguezart.com/
IG: mayaguezart

Michael Roud
www.michaelroud.com

Mike Quain
www.quainphoto.com/
IG: quainphoto

Natalie Young
www.natalieyoungla.com

Pancho Moore
No information available at this time

Paul Smith
www.paulsmithphotography.com/
IG: paulsmithphotography

Peter Konerko
www.peterkonerko.com
IG: petekonerko

Shandon Youngclaus
www.shandonphotography.com

Stephanie Girard
www.stephgirardheadshots.com
IG: stephgirardphoto

Will Catlett
www.willcatlett.com
IG: willcatlett

New York

Anthony Grasso
www.anthonygrasso.net

Chris Macke
www.mackephotography.com/

David Noles
www.davidnoles.com/

Jeremy Folmer
www.jeremyfolmer.com/

Jordan Matter
www.jordanmatter.com/

Martin Bensten and Samatha Rayward
www.cityheadshots.com/

Paul Gregory
www.paulgregoryphotography.com/

Peter Hurley
www.peterhurley.com/

Rod Goodman
www.rodgoodmanphoto.com

Sam Khan
www.imageworksnyc.com/

Atlanta

Aiva Genys
www.agpicture.com/

Carlisle Kellam
www.ckheadshotsatlanta.com

Dwayne Boyd
dwayneboydphotography.com/

Michael Justice
www.hollywoodheadshots.info/

Richard Shinn
www.rshinnphoto.com

The Buckhead Studio
www.thebuckheadstudio.com

Louisiana

Jackson (LA/ATL/NYC)
www.magazinestheadshots.com

Ken Weingart
www.edgyheadshots.com

Chicago

Aaron Gang
www.aarongang.com

Janna Giacoppo
www.jannagiacoppo.com

Naiyah Scaife (CHI/LA)
IG: NaiyahsHeadshots
E: naiyah.dream@gmail.com

Popio Stumpf
www.popiostumpf.com

Zoe Mckenzie
www.zoemckenziephotography.com

Philadelphia

Christopher Kadish
www.kadishphoto.com/hollywoodheadshots.html

Kim Carson
www.kimcarsonphotography.com

Martin Bentsen
www.cityheadshots.com
Whitney Thomas
www.whitneythomas.com

Additional Resource

www.Thumbtack.com - Search for photographers in your area. Search "Photographer" choose Headshot photography when prompted then continue to answer the questionnaire to find photographers in your area.

Submission Sites

The sites below are for the major markets but do your research for the REPUTABLE sites in your area or town. Remember you can physically drop off or mail headshots as well so be sure to research the reputable CD's in your area.

CRACKING THE ACTING CODE

Nationwide

Actors Access
www.ActorsAccess.com

Now Casting
www.NowCasting.com

Backstage
www.Backstage.com

Casting Frontier
www.CastingFrontier.com

IMDB Pro
https://Pro-labs.Imdb.com

Actors Equity
www.ActorsEquity.org

Playbill
www.Playbill.com

iActor
www.SagAftra.org/iactor-online-casting

Atlanta

800 Casting
www.800Casting.com

Chicago

Performink
www.Perform.ink

League of Chicago Theatres
www.LeagueOfChicagoTheatres.org

Los Angeles

LA Casting
www.LACasting.com

CAZT
www.Cazt.com

New York

NYCastings
www.NYcastings.com

Casting Networks
www.CastingNetworks.com

San Diego

Actors Alliance of San Diego
www.ActorsAlliance.org

San Francisco

Casting Networks
https://home.sfcasting.com

International

Casting Workbook (Canada)
www.castingworkbook.com

e-Talenta (Europe)
www.e-talenta.eu

Spotlight (UK)
www.spotlight.com

Equity (UK)
www.equity.org.uk/home

AT2 (Australia)
www.at2casting.com

Showcast (Australia, New Zealand)

www.showcast.com.au

Casting Networks International (Australia,

United Kingdom, France, India, Latin America, Russia)
https://home.castingnetworks.com

ALWAYS check with your local film commission for projects that are coming to your area. Here's a database of film commissions to search http://afci.org/film-commissions.

Here's a little industry secret when self-submitting on www.actorsaccess.com. Add a reel, slate video or clips of a special skill to your profile! Submissions are prioritized when received by casting directors. Actors with "video" attached to their profile move to the top of the list received by casting directors. Here's how submissions are prioritized: if you have a video AND slate shot you'll be seen in the 1st group received by casting, if you only have a video and no slate shot you'll be seen in the 2nd group, if you have a slate shot ONLY you'll be seen in the 3rd group, and lastly if you have no footage at all you will be seen in the 4th group.

Competitions

ABC Discovers
www.abcdiscovers.com

CBS Diversity
www.cbscorporation.com/diversity/

NBC Diversity
www.NBCUniTips.com/nbc-scene-showcase/

NBC Star Project
www.Abff.com/star-project/

Next TV Entertainment
www.NexTVEntertainment.com/acting_competition.php

Indi
www.Indi.com

Acting Hour
www.ActingHour.com/competitions.html

www.CrackingTheActingCode.com

Factbook.com/CrackingTheActingCode

Twitter: @CrackActingCode

Instagram: @CrackingTheActingCode